HAVING CONFIDENCE MEANS BELIEVING IN YOURSELF, KNOWING THAT YOU CAN HANDLE ANYTHING.

IT'S TRUSTING YOU WILL LEARN AND GROW FROM WHATEVER LIFE MIGHT BRING.

IT IS KNOWING YOU'RE AMAZING NO MATTER WHAT PEOPLE SAY, AND UNDERSTANDING THAT NO ONE HAS THE POWER TO TAKE YOUR HAPPINESS AWAY.

It makes you feel amazing and motivated to achieve. You can do hard and scary things - you just need to believe...

You already have this superpower ready to use inside of you.

Read on to find ways to grow in confidence and discover the magic it can do!

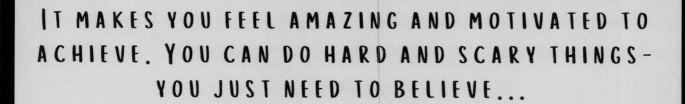

Having a superhero mindset means realising your brain power can grow.
Mistakes and challenges are exciting ways to add to what you know.

When you have one you can reach all the goals and dreams you want to,
by putting in the time and practice and not giving up until you do.

With a superhero mindset you'll know you always have the power to problem solve and be filled with tons of confidence knowing there's nothing you can't resolve.

Villain vs Superhero

WITH A VILLAIN MINDSET YOU'LL WANT TO GIVE UP EVERYTIME SOMETHING HARD COMES ALONG.

YOU CAN DEFEAT IT BY USING YOUR SUPERHERO MINDSET TO PROVE IT WRONG.

Villain mindset

"I CAN'T DO THIS."

"I GIVE UP."

"THIS IS TOO HARD."

"EVERYONE'S BETTER THAN ME AT THIS."

"I'M NOT GOOD AT THIS."

VS

Superhero mindset

"I CAN INCREASE MY BRAIN POWER."

"I CAN GET BETTER AT THIS BY PUTTING IN MORE TIME AND EFFORT."

"I CAN ASK FOR HELP WHEN I NEED IT."

"I CAN'T DO THIS **YET**."

"I WILL FOCUS ON MY OWN PROGRESS."

Real-life examples

More...

Villain mindset

THERE'S NO POINT ME DOING GYMNASTICS, I TRIED IT AND I WASN'T AS GOOD AS THE OTHER PEOPLE THERE.

MY TEACHER TOLD ME I NEED TO IMPROVE MY HANDWRITING TO GET MY PEN LICENCE. SHE SHOWED ME THE CORRECT WAY TO JOIN UP LETTERS, IT'S GOING TO TAKE ME FOREVER TO LEARN. I'LL NEVER GET MY LICENCE.

Superhero mindset

I AM A BEGINNER SO I WON'T BE AS GOOD AS PEOPLE WHO HAVE PRACTISED AND PUT IN MORE TIME AND EFFORT. I WILL FOCUS ON MY OWN PROGRESS AND BE INSPIRED BY OTHER PEOPLES SUCCESS.

I'M GRATEFUL MY TEACHER SHOWED ME THE RIGHT WAY, IT WILL HELP ME TO IMPROVE. THIS WAY MIGHT EVEN BE EASIER FOR ME AND HELP ME ACHIEVE MY GOAL FASTER.

Villain mindset

I CAN'T FINISH THIS LEVEL IN THE GAME. I KEEP DOING IT WRONG. I GIVE UP!

I DON'T WANT TO TAKE PART IN THE ASSEMBLY, WHAT IF I GET IT ALL WRONG AND LOOK SILLY.

I WANT TO JOIN THE SCHOOL FOOTBALL TEAM BUT I'M SCARED PEOPLE WILL THINK I'M RUBBISH AT IT.

Superhero mindset

MISTAKES HELP ME LEARN WHAT NOT TO DO. I CAN TAKE A BREAK AND TRY AGAIN LATER.

AS LONG AS I TRY MY BEST I'LL BE PROUD. I CAN CHOOSE TO HAVE FUN AND LAUGH AT MYSELF

IF THIS IS SOMETHING I WANT TO DO, I CAN FIND A WAY TO WORK THROUGH THE FEAR.

YOU CAN ALWAYS ASK A GROWN-UP FOR HELP TO CHANGE YOUR MINDSET!

Face your fears!

It's important to face some fears to make your confidence grow. Fear is an enormous feeling so take it as slow as you need to go.

Even heroes feel fear but they work through it to save the day. Use a superhero mindset to feel brave and make fear fade away.

Focus on your breath instead of your fear.

Fear can make your heart race so taking some big deep breaths can help you to calm down.

Try this!

Superheros Help Others

Thinking about how other people might be feeling and how you could help them, can help you forget about your own fear.

PLUS: Being kind feels good!

...CONFIDENT PEOPLE STILL MAKE MISTAKES THEY JUST KNOW THERE'S NO REASON TO BE SAD, MISTAKES ARE CHANCES TO LEARN AND GROW, THEY'RE REASONS TO BE GLAD!

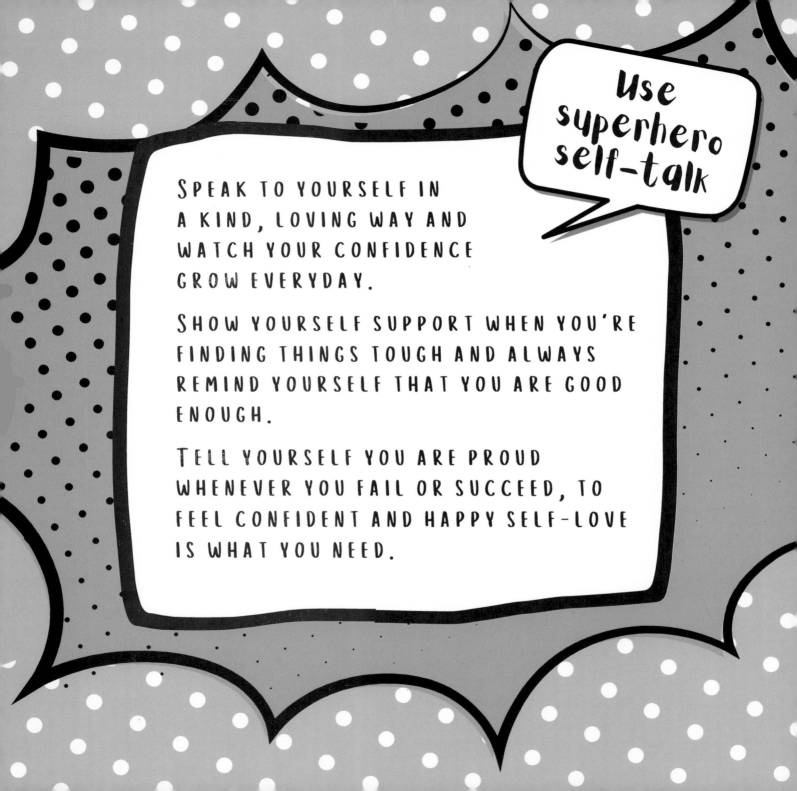

Make a plan

PLANNING HOW YOU'LL FACE A CHALLENGE CAN HELP YOU FEEL LESS SCARED. YOU WILL FEEL MORE CONFIDENT DOING SOMETHING IF YOU MAKE SURE YOU'RE PREPARED!

IT CAN BE HELPFUL TO HAVE A BACK UP PLAN READY IN CASE SOMETHING DOESN'T GO THE WAY YOU HOPED IT WOULD.
THEN YOU WON'T LOSE FAITH IN YOUR MISSION, YOU'LL STAY CONFIDENT AND KEEP MOVING FORWARD.

Break down your goals into smaller more achievable steps.

Tip 1

CREATE AN ACTION PLAN

E.G.

GOAL: SING IN FRONT OF MY FRIENDS

I'LL PREPARE AND PRACTICE A SONG UNTIL I FEEL LIKE I'VE LEARNT IT ☑

I WILL SING THE SONG IN FRONT OF A MIRROR ☑

I WILL PERFORM IT FOR MY MUM ☑

I WILL DO A PERFORMANCE FOR MY FAMILY ☑

I WILL SING IT FOR MY FRIENDS IN OUR PLAYTIME TALENT SHOW ☑

Tip 2

USE A LADDER TO DRAW OUT THE SMALLER STEPS NEEDED TO REACH YOUR MAIN GOAL!

Practice!

THE MORE YOU PRACTICE SOMETHING THE MORE CONFIDENT AT IT YOU'LL BECOME. YOU PROBABLY WON'T BE AMAZING AT SOMETHING IF YOU'VE ONLY JUST BEGUN.

YOUR ABILITIES CAN GROW THE MORE HARD WORK AND TIME YOU PUT IN. IF THERE'S SOMETHING YOU WANT TO GET BETTER AT DON'T QUIT, KEEP PRACTICING.

KEEP USING YOUR SUPERPOWER... CONFIDENCE. WITH PRACTICE IT WILL GET STRONGER!

Practice = Progress!

KEEP TRACK OF ALL THE PROGRESS YOU'RE MAKING AND NOTICE HOW CONFIDENT YOU GET!

DISCOVER THE POWER OF POSITIVITY...

No thoughts or feelings are bad to have, some just need rearranging. Use the power of positivity whenever you need your mood changing.

Have you noticed that when you're in a good mood you feel capable of more.

Do your best to focus on the positive and watch your confidence soar.

POSITIVE THINKING MEANS FOCUSING ON THE GOOD IN ANY SITUATION.

Play the reframe game

YES... → BUT

YES, I GOT A QUESTION WRONG IN CLASS...	BUT, IT MEANT I LEARNT SOMETHING NEW AND SOME OF MY CLASSMATES DID TOO!
YES, I GOT THE LOWEST SCORE IN THE CLASS...	BUT, I DID BETTER THAN I DID LAST WEEK, SO I'M MAKING PROGRESS.
YES, I MISSED A GOAL THAT COULD HAVE WON THE GAME FOR US...	BUT, I TRIED MY BEST AND STILL HAD FUN PLAYING.

You are powerful, unique and special no matter what...

That is something YOU CAN NEVER LOSE.

Even when you're not feeling your best you still have superpowers inside ready to use...

So when different things come along in life that make your confidence feel under attack, know you always have what you need to get yourself back on track.

wield a superhero shield

KEEP A SUPERHERO SHIELD UP FOR WORDS OR ACTIONS MEANT TO BE HURTFUL.
IT'S MORE IMPORTANT WHAT YOU THINK ABOUT YOURSELF, THAN WHAT OTHERS THINK OF YOU.

YOU CAN'T CONTROL HOW OTHERS BEHAVE BUT YOU CAN CONTROL HOW YOU REACT.
WHATEVER ANYONE DOES OR SAYS KNOW YOU ARE AMAZING AND THAT'S A <u>FACT</u>.

Friend VS Foe

FRIENDS WHO ARE ALWAYS THERE FOR YOU CAN
MAKE YOUR CONFIDENCE GROW.

KEEP YOUR SUPERHERO SHIELD UP FOR ANYONE
THAT WOULD RATHER KEEP IT LOW.

SURROUND YOURSELF WITH PEOPLE THAT BIG
YOU UP AND MAKE YOU FEEL GREAT!
THERE WILL BE PEOPLE THAT LOVE EXACTLY WHO
YOU ARE, TRUE FRIENDS ARE WORTH THE WAIT.

It's important to put your happiness first sometimes and not just do what makes other people happy.

You have the right to...

→ Say no
→ Say you don't like something
→ Ask questions
→ Make mistakes
→ Have a different opinion to someone else

Feeling confident enough to say how you feel might take time, but you can pair what you want with kindness.

E.G.

"No, thank you."

"I like this game but could you give me a little more space please."

"Thanks for asking, but I'd rather play alone right now."

"I love being your best friend but I'd like to play with other people too."

"The music is too loud for my ears, could you turn it down a bit please."

Don't compare...

EVERYONE IS DIFFERENT AND ON THEIR OWN SPECIAL JOURNEY TOO, IT REALLY IS IMPOSSIBLE TO COMPARE YOURSELF TO ANYONE BUT YOU!

SO ALWAYS DO YOUR BEST, FOLLOW YOUR DREAMS AND DO WHAT MAKES YOU HAPPY.

IT DOESN'T MATTER WHAT ANYONE ELSE IS DOING JUST BE THE BEST YOU THAT YOU CAN BE.

Be your own competition!

Focus on your own progress and achievements.

It's you versus you..

Can you do better than your last try❓

Have your own goals and interests...

WHAT DO YOU ENJOY LEARNING❓

DO YOU HAVE A FAVOURITE HOBBY❓

WHAT SKILLS ARE YOU WORKING TOWARDS❓

Remember...

IT'S OKAY TO FOLLOW YOUR OWN PATH.

DO WHAT YOU WANT OR ENJOY, EVEN IF THAT IS DIFFERENT FROM EVERYONE ELSE.

Quick power boosts...

Sometimes you might need a boost of confidence fast. Here are some ideas to give you a super powerful blast.

Times your confidence might need a power boost

When...
- Doing something new
- Talking in front of people
- Sticking up for yourself
- Saying no
- Facing a fear

Use to feel instantly more powerful!

Power Pose

Send your confidence from zero to hero with this strong power pose.

1 Stand or sit up straight - make your body as tall as you can

2 Push your shoulders back and your chest out

3 Lift your head high and keep your chin up

4 Stay in this pose until you feel like a powerful superhero ready to take on anything!

+ To feel even more powerful you could imagine yourself standing with your hands on your hips, wearing a superhero costume and cape.

Thinking powerful thoughts can fill you with confidence.

Superhero slogans

Use these power boosting superhero slogans or come up with your own!

"I am confident and strong"
"I am powerful"
"I am brave"
"I can do anything"
"I believe in myself"

BONUS

Other ways to boost confidence fast.

- Take BIG deep breaths
- Smile
- Listen to a song that always fills you with energy and makes you feel great.

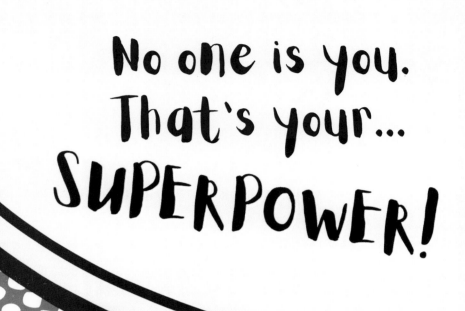

Love yourself no matter what and true confidence will come.

You are amazing as you are. You don't need to change for anyone.

Love yourself no matter what happens in your day. Be there for yourself and you will overcome anything that comes your way.

Printed in Great Britain
by Amazon